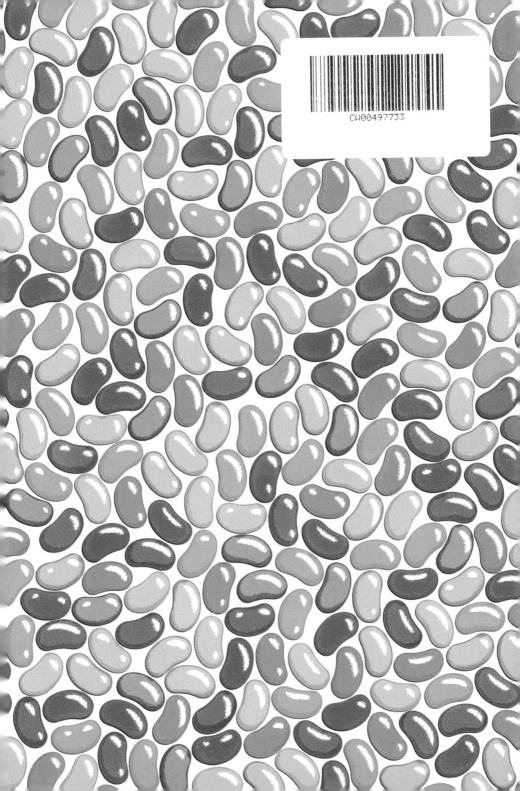

SPILL the BEANS

100 SILLY SAYINGS & PECULIAR PHRASES

Published by Collins
An imprint of HarperCollins Publishers
Westerhill Road
Bishopbriggs
Glasgow G64 2QT

www.collins.co.uk

HarperCollins Publishers
Macken House
39/40 Mayor Street Upper
Dublin 1
D01 C9W8
Ireland

First Edition 2024

© HarperCollins Publishers 2024

Collins® is a registered trademark of HarperCollins Publishers Ltd

Illustrations © Julia Murray 2024

A catalogue record for this book is available from the British Library.

ISBN 978-0-00-868829-5

Printed in India

10 9 8 7 6 5 4 3 2 1

ACKNOWLEDGEMENTS
Publisher: Beth Ralston • Editor: Kerry Ferguson
Designer: Kevin Robbins • Illustrator and Typesetter: Julia Murray
With special thanks to Maree Airlie, Alice Arthur and Emily Mercer

This book is for you if...

...you've ever heard a peculiar phrase and wondered why we say it.

Chances are, these phrases are idioms – sneaky sayings that don't mean what they *sound like* they mean. Idioms are one of the reasons why English is so fascinating, turning words into secret codes that you have to crack! Once you do, you'll be able to express yourself in new and creative ways.

In these pages, you will find all sorts of these extraordinary expressions – some funny, some fancy, some downright fantastical – alongside what they mean and the strange stories behind them.

Do you know what it means to spill the beans?
Or why we say fingers crossed?
Who let the cat out of the bag?
How do you steal someone's thunder?
And is there really an elephant in the room?

You're about to find out...

SPOT THE SAYINGS

Did you work out the sayings from the cover?

spill the beans
(page 11)

like two peas
in a pod
(page 14)

the early bird
catches the
worm
(page 26)

wear your
heart on your
sleeve
(page 80)

as fit as
a fiddle
(page 116)

eager
beaver
(page 29)

go down a
rabbit hole
(page 34)

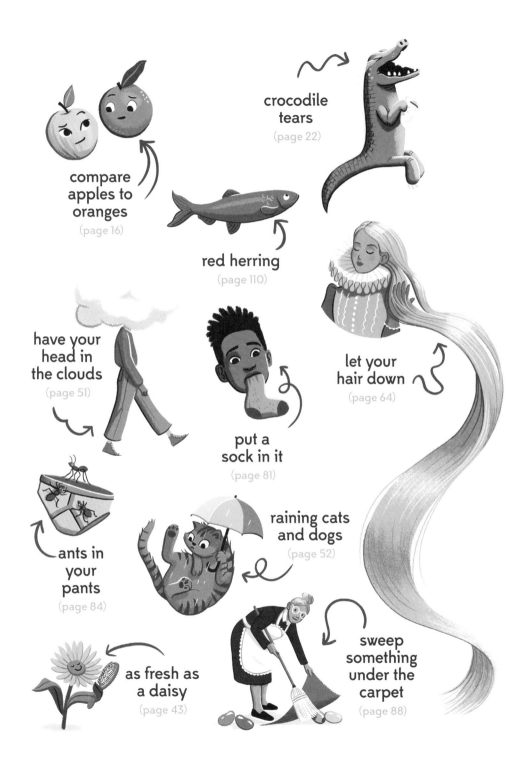

crocodile tears
(page 22)

compare apples to oranges
(page 16)

red herring
(page 110)

have your head in the clouds
(page 51)

let your hair down
(page 64)

put a sock in it
(page 81)

ants in your pants
(page 84)

raining cats and dogs
(page 52)

as fresh as a daisy
(page 43)

sweep something under the carpet
(page 88)

Contents

CLOTHING

Ants in pants! Rabbits in hats! These funny phrases are all dressed up.

HOME

Snug as a bug in a rug? You don't have to leave the house to decode these idioms.

COLOURS

You'll be tickled pink by all the colourful expressions in English.

MUSIC

Have a ball with the musical phrases in this tuneful chapter.

SPORT

Whether it's baseball, basketball, golf or cricket, sporty sayings are a slam dunk.

FOOD

have your cake and eat it

If someone says you can't have your cake and eat it, they mean that you can't get the benefits of two different situations or things – you should only get the benefit of one of them.

This confusing phrase first appeared in the English language in the 16th century, and similar sayings are found in other languages too. In Germany, they say *du kannst nicht auf zwei Hochzeiten gleichzeitig tanzen*, which means 'you can't dance at two weddings at the same time'.

spill the beans

If you spill the beans, you accidentally tell someone something that was meant to be kept a secret.

This saying is thought to come from a voting system used in ancient Greece. The story goes that each person was handed two beans and would place one in a jar to cast their vote – a light-coloured bean for a 'yes' vote or a dark-coloured bean for 'no'. If someone spilled the beans early, on purpose or by mistake, the result would be spoiled.

go pear-shaped

If you say that a situation has gone pear-shaped, you mean that things have started to go a bit wrong.

One story suggests that this saying comes from the Royal Air Force in the 1940s. If a pilot did a poor job of tracing loops in the sky, instead of being perfectly circular, they looked pear-shaped.

sour grapes

If you describe someone's attitude as sour grapes, you mean that they are pretending that they dislike something because they secretly want it but cannot have it.

This saying comes from an old Greek tale about a frustrated fox who sees some juicy grapes hanging from the branches of a tall tree. When the fox discovers he can't reach them, he sulks off, grumbling that the grapes were probably sour anyway.

like two peas
in a pod

If you describe two people as
being like two peas in a pod, you
mean that they are very similar to
each other, especially in appearance.

Dating back to the 16th century, this expression
comes from the fact that two peas inside
the same pod look identical.

dog's dinner

If you describe something as looking like a dog's dinner or a dog's breakfast, you mean that it is very messy.

This sloppy saying comes from the early 20th century and refers to the unappealing scraps a dog might be given to eat. If you've ever seen a dog eating enthusiastically, this expression makes a lot of sense!

15

compare apples to oranges

If someone says you are comparing apples to oranges, they mean that you are comparing two very different things that shouldn't be compared in the first place.

This phrase can be traced back to 1670 where it appeared in author John Ray's collection of common sayings – originally it was 'apples to oysters', which are even more different!

easy peasy lemon squeezy

If you say something is easy peasy lemon squeezy,
you are saying that it is extremely easy or simple.

It is believed that this phrase came from a British advert in
the 1950s for washing-up liquid, which was lemon-scented
and came in a squeezy bottle.

butter someone up

If someone butters you up, they are especially nice to you because they want something from you.

This saying likely comes from the ancient Hindu tradition of throwing balls of ghee (a type of butter used in Indian cooking) at statues of gods, in the hope of receiving good fortune in return.

apple of your eye

If you say that someone is the apple of your eye, you mean that they are very important to you and you are extremely fond of them.

This expression was once used to describe a part of the body. In the 16th century, the word 'pupil' (the black circle in the middle of your eye) hadn't been invented yet, so people referred to it as the 'apple of the eye' – simply because it was round and looked like an apple! Shakespeare, a famous playwright from this time period, used this saying in his comedy play, *A Midsummer Night's Dream*.

ANIMALS

crocodile tears

If you say that someone is crying crocodile tears, you think that they are only pretending, and their sadness or sympathy is not real.

There is an ancient belief that crocodiles cry tears of sadness while devouring their prey. Though they do cry, it has nothing to do with emotion. Crocodiles hiss and huff a lot while eating, which causes their eyes to water.

pigs might fly

If you say pigs might fly after someone says that something might happen, you are emphasising that you think it is extremely unlikely.

This silly saying comes from a book published in 1616, in which English author John Withals wrote: 'Pigs fly in the air with their tails forward'. In this description, pigs are not only flying, but also going backwards – which is even sillier than the modern-day version!

elephant in the room

If you announce that there is an elephant in the room, you are saying there is an obvious problem, but everyone is ignoring it.

In an old story called 'The Inquisitive Man', written in 1814 by Russian writer Ivan Krylov, a man goes to a museum and notices all sorts of small objects – but he somehow fails to spot a very large elephant in the corner! That's where this whimsical expression comes from.

let the cat out of the bag

If you let the cat out of the bag, you reveal something secret, often without meaning to.

This phrase is believed to date back to medieval markets, when untrustworthy traders would sometimes swap a piglet for a kitten, which would have been less valuable. When the poor buyer later opened the bag, the trick would be found out.

the early bird
catches the worm

If you say that the early bird catches the worm,
you mean that the person who arrives in a place
first is most likely to get what they want.

This phrase came into use in the early 17th century when it
featured in a book of English expressions by writer William
Camden. The idea behind it is simple – just as the bird who
wakes the earliest has the best chance of a tasty snack, the
person who wastes no time has the best chance of success.

hold your horses

If you tell someone to hold their horses, you are telling them to wait, slow down, or stop for a moment – usually when they are about to do something silly.

This saying comes from a time before cars existed, when horses were a common type of transport. Riders would be told to 'hold their horses' in order to stop or slow down.

frog in your throat

If you say that you have a frog in your throat, you mean that you are finding it difficult to speak clearly because of a cough or a sore throat.

In medieval times, it was believed that if you drank water containing frogspawn, the frogs would grow inside your body. People thought that sore throats and coughing could be caused by the frogs trying to escape from your tummy through your throat!

eager beaver

Someone who is described as an eager beaver is very enthusiastic about work, or very keen to please other people.

This catchy expression comes from the fact that beavers are known for their hard work, as they spend a lot of time building shelters and dams.

the bee's knees

If you say that someone or something is the bee's knees, you mean that they are absolutely wonderful.

First appearing in the English language in 1922, this sweet saying may refer to the way in which bees carry pollen on their back legs. To remove the pollen, they have to do lots of wiggling and bending of their 'knees'!

get someone's goat

If you get someone's goat, you annoy them very much.

Coming from the United States of America (USA), the story goes that this saying is from horse-racing. Goats were put in the same stable as racehorses, as they seemed to have a calming effect. If someone stole the goat, the horses would get nervous, and they wouldn't race well.

NATURE

go down a rabbit hole

If you find yourself going down a rabbit hole, you are becoming more and more interested in something, and you cannot help yourself from finding out more about it.

This curious expression comes from Lewis Carroll's 1865 classic tale, *Alice's Adventures in Wonderland*. In the opening chapter, 'Down the Rabbit Hole', Alice follows the White Rabbit into his burrow, which transports her to the weird world of Wonderland.

over the moon

If you say that you are over the moon, you mean that you are very pleased about something.

This is a simple form of the saying 'to jump over the moon', which is a line from the popular nursery rhyme 'Hey Diddle Diddle' about the cow that jumped over the moon, dating back to at least the 18th century.

make a mountain out of a molehill

If someone says that you are making a mountain out of a molehill, they mean that you are overreacting and making a big deal out of a small problem.

This idiom has appeared in English since the 16th century and there are similar sayings in many other European languages as well. In France, they say *faire d'une mouche un éléphant*, which means 'to make an elephant out of a fly'!

the tip of
the iceberg

If you say that something is the tip of the iceberg, you mean that it is only a small, noticeable part of a much bigger problem.

Taking inspiration from Mother Nature, this saying refers to the fact that only a small portion of an iceberg is visible above the water. In fact, about 90 per cent of an iceberg's mass will be below the surface!

between a rock and a hard place

If you are stuck between a rock and a hard place, you are having to choose between two equally unpleasant options.

The roots of this expression can be found all the way back in ancient Greece. In the epic poem *The Odyssey*, the hero Odysseus must pass between Scylla, a six-headed creature living in a cliff (the 'rock') and Charybdis, a sea-monster in a giant whirlpool (the 'hard place'). A tricky decision indeed!

nip something in the bud

If you nip something in the bud, you stop a bad situation or bad behaviour at an early stage, before it can get any worse.

This is a gardening term that has blossomed into everyday use. When a leaf or a flower is about to form, it is just a small bud – if you cut it, or 'nip it', then it won't grow.

a needle in a haystack

If you are searching for something and say that it is like looking for a needle in a haystack, you mean that it is going to be extremely difficult to find.

This phrase is nearly 500 years old, first appearing in the works of Irish writer Sir Thomas Moore. It has stood the test of time as it paints a perfect picture of a near-impossible task – imagine *actually* trying to find a needle in a haystack!

bark up the wrong tree

If someone says that you are barking up the wrong tree, they mean that you are making the wrong choice.

This expression dates back to early 19th-century America, when people used packs of dogs for hunting. Sometimes particularly sneaky animals, like racoons, would trick dogs into thinking they were up a certain tree, making them bark – when in fact they had escaped!

a breath of fresh air

If you say that something or someone is a breath of fresh air, you are saying that they are pleasantly different from what you are used to.

This phrase likely comes from the 18th century, when people were unhappy about the poor quality of the air during the Industrial Revolution – a time when people started making things using machines in factories, instead of by hand. Leaving these polluted areas was, therefore, a breath of fresh air.

as fresh as a daisy

If you say that you are as fresh as a daisy, you mean that you feel bright, alert and full of energy.

In Old English, daisies were referred to as the 'day's eye' because their petals close over at night and reopen in the morning. The petals look like eyelashes, while the yellow circle in the middle looks like the eye itself. So, 'fresh as a daisy' came to mean that someone had a good night's sleep.

43

reach for the stars

If you reach for the stars, you are being very ambitious and trying hard to achieve a goal, even though it may be difficult.

This saying comes from a very old poem in Latin (an ancient language) which had the line *sic itur ad astra*, meaning 'so one journeys to the stars'. This eventually turned into the simpler modern-day expression.

hit the hay

If you say that you are going to hit the hay or hit the sack, you mean that you are going to bed.

These phrases have been used since the early 19th century when sacks were stuffed with hay to make mattresses – so lying down in bed really was hitting the hay. Thankfully, mattresses are much more comfortable nowadays!

WEATHER

take a rain check

If you ask to take a rain check on an invitation, you are politely declining the offer for now, but you might accept it another time.

This saying comes from sporting competitions in the USA, where a rain check was an actual ticket given to spectators to see another baseball game if the original game they came to see was rained off. Now we use this phrase for all sorts of events.

come rain or shine

If you say that you will do something come rain or shine, you mean that you will do it regardless of the circumstances, and whatever the weather.

Entering the English language in the 17th century, this expression likely comes from farming, as farmers have to tend to their crops and care for their animals in all weather conditions – not just when the sun is shining!

steal someone's thunder

If someone steals your thunder, they stop you from getting attention or praise by doing something better or more exciting.

In the early 18th century, British playwright John Dennis invented a device for making the sound of thunder for his new play – but the show was unsuccessful and soon closed. Shortly afterwards, Dennis went to see another play performed in the same theatre, when he heard the sound of his device booming across the stage. Feeling cheated, Dennis jumped up and dramatically accused them of stealing his thunder!

have your head
in the clouds

If you have your head in the clouds, it means that you are not paying attention, and are instead daydreaming about things that are impractical or impossible.

This expression comes from the mid-17th century. This was before the invention of aeroplanes, so the sky was well and truly out of reach for humans. Having your head in the clouds was *actually* impossible.

raining cats and dogs

If someone says it is raining cats and dogs, they mean it is raining very heavily.

In Norse mythology (old stories that were once told in Scandinavian countries), cats and dogs were linked with the spirit of the storm and could change the weather. Odin, the Norse god of storms, was often accompanied by dogs and wolves, which were symbols of wind – while witches would ride their brooms during heavy rain, alongside their trusty black cats.

on cloud nine

If you say that you are on cloud nine, you mean that you are very, very happy.

This expression likely comes from the numbered cloud categories that weather forecasters used in the 19th century. The ninth cloud, called 'cumulonimbus', is the highest and reaches up to 30,000 feet. It is also the fluffiest and most comfortable-looking – the kind of cloud you'd be happy to lounge on!

every cloud has a silver lining

If you say that every cloud has a silver lining, you mean that every sad or unpleasant situation has a positive side to it.

Since the 17th century, this hopeful expression has been used to comfort people who are going through a tough time. It brings to mind an image of the sun bursting through a rain cloud, making it look as if the cloud is glowing.

chase rainbows

If you are chasing rainbows, you are wasting your time trying to get something that you can never have.

This expression comes from the old tale of finding a pot of gold at the end of the rainbow – which, sadly, is just wishful thinking! In the 19th century, people who were pursuing unrealistic or fanciful goals were called 'rainbow chasers'.

snowball effect

A snowball effect is a situation where something starts out small but grows in size or importance, quickly getting out of control.

This expression is an analogy (a comparison between one thing and another). It refers to the way in which a snowball collects snow as it rolls down a hill, getting bigger and bigger as it goes.

break the ice

If you break the ice, you remove the awkwardness from a social situation, often by making a joke.

This saying comes from the Arctic expeditions of the late 19th century, when special ships were built to break the ice and allow explorers to pass. The analogy here is that, just as breaking the ice helps ships sail through the water, breaking the ice at parties helps conversation flow freely!

WEATHER

under the weather

If you say that you are under the weather, you mean that you feel slightly unwell.

This saying comes from the days of old sailing ships. When a sailor became ill or seasick, often because of stormy weather, they were sent below decks to the sheltered part of the ship to recover. This was considered to be 'under the weather'!

the calm before
the storm

If you describe a period of time as being the calm before the storm, you mean that it is very quiet and peaceful now, but there will soon be lots of activity, noise or chaos.

This idiom was originally used by sailors to describe a real weather event observed at sea – before a storm hit, the air would become strangely still. Nowadays, it is used for all sorts of situations, often as a warning.

BODY

bury your head in the sand

If you bury your head in the sand,
you are refusing to face a problem or accept
the truth about something unpleasant.

This expression comes from the mistaken belief that
ostriches bury their heads in the sand when they are in
danger, which wouldn't be a very good way to hide from
predators! They actually dig their heads in sand to make
nests for their eggs.

sweet tooth

If you say that you have a sweet tooth,
you mean that you like to eat things
that are sugary and sweet.

In the Middle Ages, this phrase was made by sticking
two common words together: 'sweet' and 'tooth'. At the
time, the word 'tooth' meant 'taste' or 'liking' – so the
phrase as a whole meant 'sweet liking'!

let your hair down

If you let your hair down, you have fun
and enjoy yourself without worrying
about what people think.

This expression dates back to the 17th century, when
women would often wear their hair up in fancy hairdos,
pulled away from their faces. Having their hair down was
unusual, and therefore seen as a much more relaxed style.

pull the wool over someone's eyes

If you pull the wool over someone's eyes, you trick them or lie to them.

In the past, wigs for men were fashionable and were sometimes called 'wool' because they looked like a sheep's fleece. If a mischief-maker pulled the wool over someone's eyes, it would stop them from being able to see and – worse – it provided an opportunity to rob them!

land on your feet

When you land on your feet, you find yourself in a good situation that is the result of luck rather than hard work.

It is often the case that when a cat falls, it will manage to land on its feet without hurting itself. This natural ability is called the 'righting reflex'.

lick into shape

If you lick something into shape,
you do everything you possibly
can to change or improve it.

This saying comes from the medieval belief
that bear cubs were born shapeless and had to
be licked into shape by their mothers.

ears are burning

If someone says that their ears are burning, they have a feeling that someone else is talking about them.

This phrase comes from the ancient Roman superstition (a belief that is not based on fact) that if someone's right ear felt like it was burning, somebody was saying nice things about them – but if their left ear was burning, they were saying nasty things!

find your feet

If you are finding your feet, you are becoming more confident and learning how to manage a new task or situation.

If you have ever seen a newborn animal wobbling its way to a standing position, you'll understand where this expression comes from!

in over your head

If you say that you are in over your head, you mean that you are involved in a situation that you find difficult to deal with.

This phrase dates back to the 16th century and is thought to come from the image of being in water that is so deep you can't keep your head above it. As very few people could swim back then, if you were out of your depth, you were in big trouble!

head over heels

If you say that you are head over heels, you mean that you are deeply in love with someone.

Until the late 18th century, this expression was the other way around – 'heels over head' – which meant being upside-down or doing a somersault. The idea is that falling in love can sweep you off your feet!

feast your eyes

If you feast your eyes on something, you look at it with wonder and enjoyment.

This expression is likely to be another one of Shakespeare's creations, featuring in 'Sonnet 47': 'With my love's picture then my eye doth feast'. It brings to mind a pair of eyes stretched wide, gazing in astonishment at something, or someone, wonderful!

play it by ear

If you say that you will play it by ear, you mean that you will deal with things as they happen, rather than making a plan.

The original meaning of this phrase was to play a tune by heart or by improvising, without looking at sheet music. From there, it came to mean other types of making it up as you go along!

fingers crossed

If you cross your fingers or have your fingers crossed, you are hoping for good luck or success.

Have you ever wondered why we cross our fingers when wishing someone well? It comes from an old superstition that making the sign of the cross will keep away bad luck!

break a leg

The expression break a leg is said to performers who are about to go on stage as a way of wishing them good luck.

This comes from one of many superstitions to do with the theatre. In this case, many actors consider it unlucky to say 'good luck', so they pretend to do the opposite and wish each other bad luck instead!

bite your tongue

If you bite your tongue, you are trying very hard to avoid saying something that you would really like to say, because it is not appropriate to say it.

This expression dates back to at least the time of Shakespeare, appearing in his history play, *Henry VI*. It refers to the fact that if you hold your tongue between your teeth, it is physically impossible to speak.

rule of thumb

A rule of thumb is a general rule about something, which is based on experience and guesswork rather than exact calculations.

Coming from the 17th century, this saying likely refers to a time when traders would use the tip of their thumb as a unit of measurement.

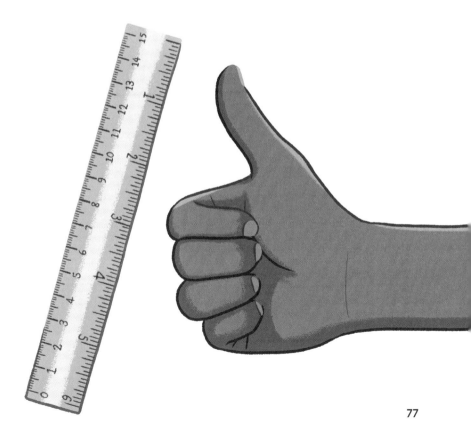

CLOTHING

wear your heart on your sleeve

If you wear your heart on your sleeve, you allow your feelings to be obvious to everyone around you.

This phrase comes from the Middle Ages when knights would take part in jousting contests – a medieval sport where two people on horseback fought each other with long, pointed weapons. The knights would wear something belonging to a lady, like a scarf, around the sleeve of their armour as a display of their love.

put a sock in it

If you tell someone to put a sock in it, you are rudely telling them to stop talking.

In the late 19th and early 20th centuries, phonographs and gramophones were popular. These old-fashioned music players amplified the sound through large horns, and woollen socks were often shoved inside the 'mouth' of the instrument to lower the volume.

have something up your sleeve

If you have something up your sleeve, you have a secret plan that you will use to your advantage when the time is right.

This sneaky saying dates back to the 16th century, when sleeves were generally larger and longer and could even be used as pockets. The expression has likely stayed in use thanks to the popular magician's trick of pulling unlikely items, like silk scarves and bouquets of flowers, from their sleeves.

pull a rabbit
out of the hat

If someone pulls a rabbit out of the hat, they find a
sudden and unexpected solution to a problem.

Another magical expression, this one refers to the iconic trick where
a magician pulls a white rabbit out of an empty top hat. French
magician Louis Comte (known as 'The King's Conjurer') was the first
to perform this trick, doing so for King Louis XVIII in 1814.

ants in your pants

If you say that someone has ants in their pants,
you mean that they are being fidgety or impatient.

This rhyming expression comes from the USA, where 'pants'
is the American word for 'trousers'. Whether it's jeans or undies,
the meaning is very clear – imagine the feeling of *actually*
having ants crawling around in your clothes!

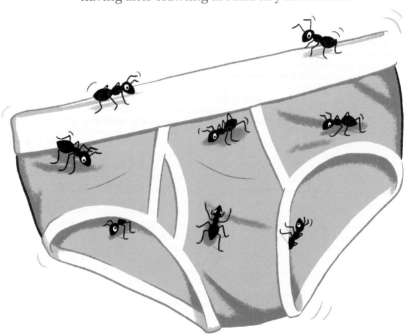

the shoe is on the other foot

If you say the shoe is on the other foot, you mean that a situation has been switched around, so that the person who was in the worse position before is now in a better one.

Believe it or not, until the end of the 18th century, shoemakers did not make 'right' and 'left' shoes – all shoes were the same and could be worn on either foot! So, if you found that one of your shoes was hurting, you could try wearing it on the other foot to see if it felt better.

HOME

sweep something under the carpet

If you sweep something under the carpet or under the rug, you try to hide or ignore a problem, in the hope that it will be forgotten.

Coming into use during the early 20th century, this saying is based on the idea of a lazy cleaner sweeping dirt under a rug, rather than cleaning it up properly with a dustpan and brush.

get out of bed on the wrong side

If you say that someone got out of bed on the wrong side, you mean that they are in a very bad mood, which will last all day long.

This relates to the old superstition that it was unlucky to put your left foot on the ground first when getting out of bed. The same was true for putting on your left shoe first!

as snug as a bug in a rug

If you say that you are as snug as a bug in a rug, you mean that you feel very comfortable and cosy.

People have been using this expression since the 18th century. It likely came from the idea of moths nesting inside a rolled-up carpet, and has probably lasted this long thanks to the cute and catchy rhyme.

on the same wavelength

If two people are on the same wavelength, they find it easy to understand each other and they tend to agree, because they share similar interests or opinions.

This saying comes from the early days of radio broadcasting, at the start of the 20th century. To be able to listen to a particular programme, people had to tune their radios to the correct frequency or wavelength.

can't hold a candle

If you say that one person or thing can't hold a candle to another, you mean that the first person or thing is not nearly as good as the second.

This saying is older than electricity! Before lightbulbs were invented, assistants had to hold candles to light the work of more experienced craftspeople. If someone couldn't hold a candle to another person, it meant that they weren't even qualified to be their assistant!

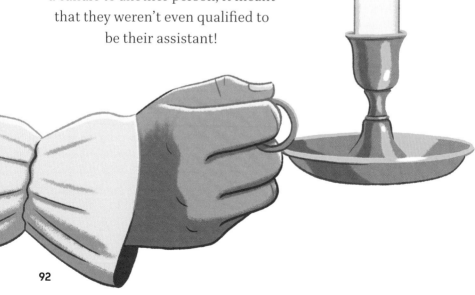

everything but the kitchen sink

If you go on holiday and bring everything but the kitchen sink, it means you packed too much and probably more than you need.

This expression comes from World War II, when many families donated their household possessions – especially those made of metal – to help with the war effort. But kitchen sinks were thought to be too heavy, so they were not included.

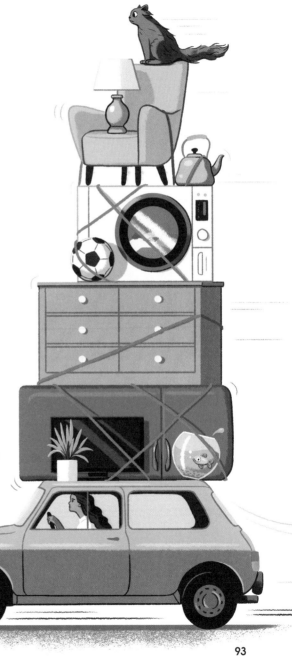

put something to bed

If you put something to bed, you successfully complete a task or solve a problem.

Surprisingly, this one doesn't have anything to do with the beds we sleep in. On an old-fashioned printing press, the bed is the flat part that holds the letters. So, when journalists talk about putting a newspaper or a magazine to bed, they mean they are sending it off to the printers.

ring a bell

If you say that something rings a bell, you mean that it feels slightly familiar to you, although you may not know why.

This expression likely comes from a famous experiment by Pavlov, a Russian psychologist (someone who studies how people and animals think and act). He trained dogs to associate the sound of a bell with food. The ringing of the bell caused the dogs to drool!

strike while the iron is hot

If you strike while the iron is hot, you act immediately, while you have the best chance of success.

This expression comes from the 15th-century art of blacksmithing (making objects from metal). Blacksmiths would soften iron (the metal, not the household appliance!) with heat before hammering it into shape. It would only stay soft for a short amount of time, so they really would have to strike while the iron was hot.

hit the nail on the head

If you hit the nail on the head, you do or say something that is exactly right.

The story behind this saying is wonderfully straightforward. It comes from carpentry (making or building things with wood), and refers to the satisfaction of hitting a nail with a hammer and getting it in exactly the right spot.

COLOURS

see red

If you say that someone sees red, you mean that they become very angry all of a sudden.

This expression comes from Spanish bullfighting, where the colour red is believed to make the bulls angry. The bullfighter, called the 'matador', waves a red cape to make the bull charge.

green fingers

If you say that someone has green fingers or green thumbs, you mean that they are very good at gardening.

Coming into use in the early 20th century, this saying sprouted from the fact that gardeners' hands often become stained green when working with plants.

tickled pink

If you say that you are tickled pink, you mean that you are extremely pleased about something.

This expression undoubtedly refers to the fact that a person being tickled will often be pink in the face from laughing so hard!

blue in the face

If you say that someone does something until they are blue in the face, you mean that however much they do it, it will not make any difference.

The image behind this frustrating phrase is of someone who is putting in so much effort into talking or arguing that they become out of breath, then turn blue from lack of oxygen!

103

green with envy

If you say that someone is green with envy,
you mean that they are very jealous.

The ancient Greeks used to believe that jealousy would
turn your skin slightly green! But it was Shakespeare who
invented the famous phrase 'green-eyed monster', which
turns the idea of envy into a living, breathing beast!

out of the blue

If you describe an event as being out of the blue or a bolt from the blue, you mean that it happened suddenly and unexpectedly.

This expression refers to an unlikely weather event – when a bolt of lightning strikes a clear blue sky. This can be dangerous, because it happens without warning!

show your true colours

If someone shows their true colours, you see what they are really like, and you discover that they are not as nice as you thought they were.

Dating back to the 18th century, this phrase is to do with flags on ships. Pirates used to trick other sailors by flying fake flags so that they would not cause suspicion – but once they raised their real flag, they revealed their 'true colours'.

pass with flying colours

If you take a test and pass with flying colours, you have done exceptionally well.

Another sailing term, this one refers to a victorious battleship, or a ship that had been successful in trade, sailing into port with its flags still flying. An unsuccessful ship, on the other hand, would lower its flags.

heart of gold

If you say that someone has a heart of gold, you mean that they are very good and kind to others.

This shiny saying has been in use since the 16th century and appeared in Shakespeare's history play, *Henry V*. The simplest and most likely explanation is that gold was, and still is, considered to be pure and precious.

once in a blue moon

If you say that something happens once in a blue moon, you mean that it happens very rarely.

When there are two full moons in the same month, the second one is called a 'blue moon'. This is a very rare event, happening only once every two or three years. Also, weirdly, blue moons aren't actually blue! They get their name from the 16th-century expression 'the Moon is blue', which was used to describe something considered to be impossible.

red herring

If you say that something is a red herring, you mean that it is not important, and it is distracting you from the main task at hand.

An actual red herring is a type of fish that has been dried and smoked, turning bright red in the process. In the past, their scent was sometimes used to distract dogs during a hunt – which is where the modern-day meaning comes from.

give the green light

If you give the green light to someone, you give them permission to do something.

This expression dates back to the late 19th century, coming from the light signals used along railroads to show when it was safe for trains to pass. It started being used more generally by the early 20th century, because that's when traffic lights started appearing on roads too.

blow your own trumpet

If someone says that you are blowing your own trumpet or horn, they mean that you are being boastful.

This phrase likely comes from medieval times, when the arrival of royalty and other important people was traditionally announced by the blowing of a trumpet or horn.

have a ball

If you say that you are having a ball, you mean that you are having a very good time.

Here, the word 'ball' is used in the sense of a formal dance. In centuries past, grand balls were hosted by high society, where a fancy meal would be followed by music and ballroom dancing.

as fit as a fiddle

If you say that you are as fit as
a fiddle (a type of violin), you mean that
you are healthy and physically fit.

When this saying was invented in the 17th century, the word
'fit' meant 'suitable' or 'fit for purpose' rather than healthy.
Since fiddles are instruments that need lots of care to be kept
in good condition – for example, by having strings replaced
regularly – that's likely where this phrase came from.

like a broken record

If you describe yourself as sounding like a broken record, you are saying that you are repeating yourself a lot.

This expression comes from the 1940s, following the invention of vinyl records. When these records got scratched, they would either skip a section of music, or repeat the same section over and over again.

MUSIC

face the music

If you face the music, you admit that you have done something wrong and you are ready to accept the consequences of your actions, however unpleasant they may be.

This expression was likely born in the theatre, where the orchestra sits in front of the stage during operas and musicals. So, when a performer faces the audience, they also face the orchestra – or 'the music'.

pay the piper

If you pay the piper, you take responsibility for your actions and suffer the consequences of careless behaviour.

You might recognise this saying from the well-known tale of *The Pied Piper of Hamelin*. The people of Hamelin agree to hire the piper to lead all the rats away from the town with his magical music. Afterwards, they refuse to pay him – so he kidnaps their children in revenge!

SPRT

hole in one

If someone describes something as being a hole in one, they mean it is a perfect achievement.

This phrase comes from golf. A hole in one is a shot that gets the golf ball into the hole on the first try, with a single stroke. Now it is also used for rare and remarkable accomplishments outside of the sporting world.

slam dunk

If you say that something is a slam dunk, you mean that it will definitely be successful.

This saying is from basketball. A slam dunk is a shot where the player jumps up high to throw the ball forcefully through the ring from above. Now we use it to describe all sorts of successes – sporty or otherwise!

SPORT

go back to square one

If you attempt a task and find yourself going back to square one, it means you have to start over from the very beginning and try again.

There are lots of theories about this phrase. It may come from old radio broadcasts of football matches, where commentators divided the pitch into 'squares' to help listeners visualise the gameplay. But it is more likely to be a reference to the popular board game Snakes and Ladders, where players sometimes land on slippery snakes that send them back to square one.

off your own bat

If someone does something off their own bat, they do it without anyone else telling or asking them to.

Coming into use in the 18th century, this sporty saying is from the game of cricket, where players score runs by hitting the ball off their own bats. The phrase 'off your own back' is actually a common mishearing of this expression.

knock it out of the park

If you say that someone knocked it out of the park, you mean that they did something extraordinarily well.

This phrase comes from the American sport of baseball, where knocking it out of the park means hitting the ball so hard that it goes out of the play area, allowing the batter to pass all the bases at once and score a home run.

cover all the bases

If you cover all the bases, you prepare for every possibility in a situation.

This is another phrase inspired by baseball, where batters have to touch all the bases (first, second, third and home) to score a run. The opposing team must therefore cover all the bases to stop that from happening.

DISCOVER A WONDERFUL WORD EVERY DAY

Never be lost for
words again...

collins.co.uk

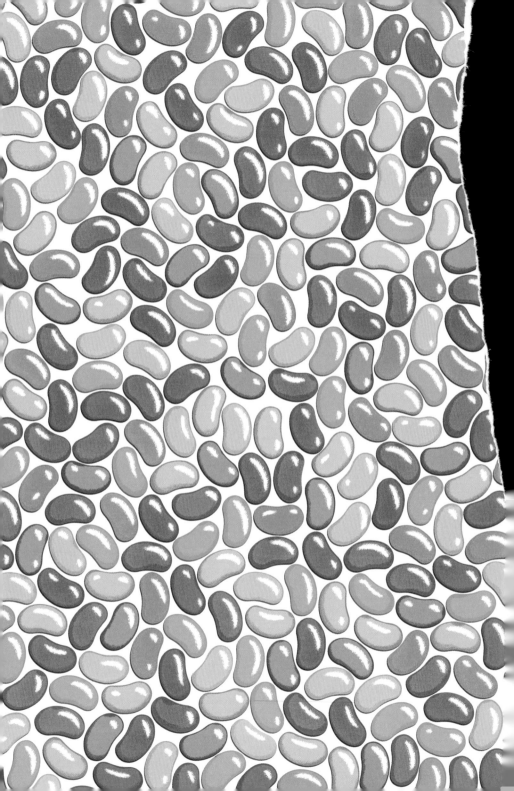